A JUST FOR A DAY BOOK

SHARK IN THE SEA

JOANNE RYDER

ILLUSTRATED BY

MICHAEL ROTHMAN

MORROW JUNIOR BOOKS / NEW YORK

The author and illustrator gratefully thank A. Peter Klimley, Ph.D., Marine Animal Behaviorist, Bodega Marine Laboratory of the University of California at Davis, for his expert help and evaluation of this work.

AUTHOR'S NOTE

It is thought that the earliest known sharks hunted the seas about 400 million years ago—nearly 200 million years before the first dinosaurs roamed the earth.

Today, the largest predatory fish is known as the great white shark, though only its underside is white. Its scientific name, *Carcharodon carcharias,* or "ragged tooth," is a more apt description. Though it may grow to a length of fifteen to twenty feet and weigh 3,000 pounds or more, a white shark's muscular body is boneless. Its skeleton is made of tough, flexible cartilage—like that in the tip of your nose. It is thought that white sharks may need to move constantly to breathe. As it swims forward, water enters its mouth and passes through its gills, filtering oxygen from the water.

White sharks swim in all the world's temperate seas. Their elevated body temperature permits them to live and hunt in cold water, unlike the majority of other sharks, which favor tropical seas. White sharks are daytime hunters, searching the shallow waters near coasts and islands for prey. Their keen senses make them amazing predators. They can smell small traces of chemicals in the water—substances that may include the blood and body fluids of injured or dead animals. Color-sensitive vision helps them track their prey. Like other fish, sharks have sensors along their sides that detect the vibrations of moving or struggling creatures. Sharks also have a unique sense that detects electrical fields emitted by other animals.

A white shark's mouth, lined with serrated triangular-shaped teeth, is a formidable weapon. Rows of spare teeth are constantly being formed to replace lost ones. Small white sharks feed on fish and other small sharks. Adult white sharks hunt seals and sea lions and scavenge on dead whales. When hunting seals, white sharks attack with one massive bite. A seal may die of blood loss while being carried in the shark's mouth. Then the shark may release the seal to float to the surface, where the shark returns to feed.

While we fear white sharks because they sometimes attack swimmers and divers, most humans survive shark attacks. Some scientists believe white sharks may prefer fatty marine mammals, and, after biting a human, they do not return to feed. Others believe that people are often rescued by companions after the initial attack and are safely away before the shark comes back.

Relatively rare and very secretive, white sharks have not survived in captivity. Scientists still have much to learn about their hidden lives, but they believe white sharks are necessary in the sea's ecology. They help preserve fish populations by preying on fish-eating seals and sea lions.

The great white shark in this book is hunting one fall day in the Pacific Ocean near the South Farallon Islands, about thirty miles west of San Francisco, California.

Acrylic paint was used for the full-color illustrations. The text type is 14-point ITC Garamond Book.

Text copyright © 1997 by Joanne Ryder. Illustrations copyright © 1997 by Michael Rothman. All rights reserved.
No part of this book may be reproduced or utilized in any form or by any means, electronic or mechanical, including photocopying, recording, or by any information storage and retrieval system, without permission in writing from the Publisher. Inquiries should be addressed to William Morrow and Company, Inc., 1350 Avenue of the Americas, New York, NY 10019.

Printed in Singapore at Tien Wah Press.

1 2 3 4 5 6 7 8 9 10

Library of Congress Cataloging-in-Publication Data
Ryder, Joanne.   Shark in the sea/Joanne Ryder; illustrated by Michael Rothman.   p. cm.—(A Just for a day book)
Summary: One fall day a great white shark, hungry and alone, glides unseen,
watching and waiting for someone unwary to become his meal.
ISBN 0-688-14909-X (trade)—ISBN 0-688-14910-3 (library)
1. White shark—Juvenile fiction. [1. White shark—Fiction. 2. Sharks—Fiction.]
I. Rothman, Michael, ill. II. Title. III. Series. PZ10.3.R954Sh 1997 [E]—dc20 [6700] 96-16963 CIP AC

Imagine
you are diving
falling
feeling air
rushing past.
You slide
into water,
wrapping your body
in coolness.
Below the surface
you swim,
eyes closed,
feet kicking
as you change....

You are sleek
and streamlined,
growing larger
and stronger.
Tiny toothlike scales
cover your skin,
cover your boneless
muscular body.
Your powerful tail—
a large crescent fin—
weaves back and forth,
pushing you forward
while other fins
steady you
as you glide.

You are a great white shark,
dark above and pale below,
a giant fish in the sea.
Other swimmers
rise to the surface,
needing air to breathe.
But you are breathing
as fish do,
your gills taking
oxygen from water.
You are a white shark,
ever swimming
ever moving forward
so water can glide
into your wide mouth
through your slitted gills
and you can breathe
in the sea.

With open, unblinking eyes
you scan the sunlit waters,
bright above and dark below.
You are a hunter,
feared and mighty—
your weapon
a gaping mouth
lined with triangles
ragged and sharp,
daggers erect
to slice and tear
and spare teeth
ever ready
to replace them.

You are a hunter,
hungry and alone.
Your keen senses
help you track
the trails of
others hidden
in the unclear
ever-flowing sea.
Cruising slowly,
you are wary—
smelling
watching
sensing
waiting
for someone
out of sight.

Vibrations dance
along your body.
First, you feel something
darting toward you.
Then you see a silver cloud,
a school of swirling fish.
Too fast for *you* to catch,
they hunt for food
too tiny for *you* to eat.
And as you swim,
fish feel you moving,
making vibrations
that dance along
their scaly skins.
Swerving from
your open mouth
your sharp teeth,
fish scatter...
just in case.

Coming closer
chasing fish,
someone sleek and agile
spins and somersaults,
looking everywhere...
                    for you.

Old scars line her brown back—
tooth marks from a slower shark.
Too wary, too watchful,
sea lion swiftly slips away.
Skimming the surface above
other sea lions race together,
leaping like dolphins,
leaping quickly out of sight.
Below them
you are hunting,
ever moving
waiting till the
time is right.

You are swimming near
an island where tall rocks
rise above cool waters
and creatures rest
along the barren shore.
Sea lions bark loudly,
louder than the crashing sea
that races toward them
wave after wave.

Along another cove
elephant seals hug
the sandy spots...
till the tide rises,
stealing the beach,
forcing them
to slip from safety
into the sea.

A young seal
swims through
the chilly waters,
warmed by
a thick layer of fat.
His rear flippers
pulse open
and closed,
pushing him onward.

He holds his breath
a long, long time,
nostrils shut tight,
but he cannot swim
underwater forever.
A breathless seal
glides up and up,
needing air.

Dangling briefly
on the surface,
seal is breathing,
never seeing
you are near.
Below,
your dark back
slides over
dark rocks.

Without warning
you soar
from below
from behind,
your crescent tail
beating
beating
in the water.
You are racing
watching
tracking
even sensing
the faint
signal
of his
beating
heart.

You lift
your snout
and stretch
your red jaws
incredibly wide,
exposing
a pale circle
of daggers
that cut
and tear
as you
bite.

Flapping gulls
hover over
a red patch
spreading
in the sea.
A tall dark fin
slices through
the redness
and disappears.

Far and below
you carry the seal,
holding him tightly
till he stops bleeding,
biting just once,
letting him go.
One bite is enough....

A still body floats,
drifting on the waves.
One dark fin draws close.
You come to claim your prey.
But...
a second fin rises, circling.
Another shark,
following a trail of scents,
has come to feed.
You lift your tail high,
slapping it on the sea,
splashing, threatening,
keeping him away.
He slaps the water
and so do you until...
one dark fin glides off,
leaving you to eat
your meal alone.

You are
a great white shark,
a fish, a giant,
ever moving
day and night,
breathing
below the surface,
hunting slyly
out of sight.
Gliding gracefully,
your dark back
your pale belly
your sleek fins
blend, fading
in the blueness
as you feel yourself
changing....

And you rise up,
stretching
leaping
breathing air,
leaving the world
of giant hunters,
ever moving
ever gliding
hidden in the sea.